THE CLASSROOM

of

CONTENTMENT

Student Book

Where You Learn That

God Is Enough

Niki Lott

Christian Compositions
Niki Lott
(724) 510-9277
www.ChristianCompositions.com

ISBN: 978-0-578-56790-7

CONTENTS

CONTENTMENT EXPLAINED

Niki Lott

INTRODUCTION

The Biblical Definition of Contentment

Consider the following statement, and try to finish it in your mind:

"I would be happy/satisfied/content if _____

_____."

Are you content? _____

If not, what do you think it would take to make you content? _____

_____

What does it even mean to truly be content? _____

_____

Contentment is defined in *Strong's Concordance of the Bible* as "to avail, be _____, be content, be _____, suffice, be sufficient".

Webster's 1828 Dictionary defines the word "content" as "Literally, held, contained within limits; hence, _____; not disturbed; having a mind ____ _____; easy; _____ so as not to repine, object, or oppose."

Compare to I Peter 3:4: "But let it be the hidden man of the _____, in that which is not _____, even the ornament of a meek and _____ _____ which is in the sight of God of great price."

According to the Bible, spiritual contentment cannot be based on the following:

_____

_____ of _____

_____ _____

**True contentment is not about _____ we possess outwardly;
it is about _____ we possess inwardly.
Contentment is simply about satisfaction with God
and His provision for me.**

Spiritual contentment also will not be characterized by these attitudes or attributes:

1. It is not _____.

    -Not _____ (Phil. 3:12)

Contentment is not _____-_____.

    -Not _____(Phil. 3:14)

Contentment is not _____-_____. (Rev. 3:17).

2. It is not _____ (I Cor. 4:1-2; I Pet. 4:10).

"Not that I speak in respect of want: for ____ _____ _____, in whatsoever state I am, therewith to be content. I know both how to be abased, and I know how to abound: every where and in all things ____ _____ _____ both to be full and to be hungry, both to abound and to suffer need. I can do all things through Christ which strengtheneth me." (Phil. 4:11-13)

Class Assignment:

Is there an area(s) where you struggle to be content? Write it down, and take the time to pray over these specific needs, and ask the Lord to teach you to be content. If you feel comfortable (and have time) to share these in your group, be sure to pray for one another.

Scripture Writing Challenge:

Scripture writing challenges will be included throughout this book as an optional way to copy and meditate on the verses in the study. You will need a separate journal or notebook to use for copying the Scriptures.

☐ I Pet. 3:4
☐ Eccl. 5:10
☐ Phil. 3:12, 14
☐ Rev. 3:17
☐ I Cor. 4:1-2
☐ I Pet. 4:10
☐ Lk. 12:19-21
☐ Phil. 4:11-13

Memory Verse: (Phil. 4:11) "Not that I speak in respect of want: for I have learned, in whatsoever state I am, therewith to be content."

LESSON 1

The Basis of Contentment

The basis of our contentment is not _____or
_____, but a _____.

Who is to be the basis of our contentment? It is _____.

Hebrews 13:5 says, "Let your conversation be without covetousness; and ____
_____ with _____ _____ _____
_____ _____: for he hath said, ___ will _____ _____
thee nor _____ thee."

_____

_____

**He says that we can be content with _____ we have because of
_____ He is.**

Question: What do you have that you cannot lose?

(Mt. 6:19-21) "Lay not up for yourselves _____ upon
_____, where moth and rust doth _____, and where thieves
break through and _____: But lay up for yourselves _____
in _____, where neither moth nor rust doth corrupt, and where
thieves do not break through nor steal: For where your _____ is, there
will your _____ be also."

If we are basing our contentment on _____ things,
then our contentment will be _____ at best.

The key question to this study is this: Is God _____?
(Ps. 73:25-26)

If you know Christ as Savior:

- You have the assurance of His _____.(Heb. 13:5)
- You have the assurance of His _____. (Phil. 4:19)
- You have the assurance of His _____. (II Tim. 1:7; Jn. 1:12)
- You have the assurance of His _____. (Jn. 14:27; Phil. 4:6-7)

Contentment is something we must learn from the Lord.

What are two ways that God teaches us?

1. Through His _____ (Pro. 22:19-21; Rom. 10:17)

2. Through His _____ (Jn. 14:26)

**"The secret is Christ in me,
not me in a different set of circumstances."**

–Elisabeth Elliott

 **Assignment:**

Spend some time thinking about who God is. List some of His attributes.

Purpose to take time each day to thank and praise God for WHO He is, not just for what He has done or for something He has given you. If you are looking for ideas, take time to read the Psalms. Many of the psalms are thanksgiving and praise to God for His character. As we learn more about our Savior, and come to know Him better, we will find it easier to trust Him, to rest in His will for us, and to be content with His plan for our lives.

Memory Verse: (Heb. 13:5) "Let your conversation be without covetousness; and be content with such things as ye have: for he hath said, I will never leave thee nor forsake thee."

Scripture Writing Challenge

- ☐ Heb. 13:5
- ☐ Ps. 73:25-26
- ☐ Phil. 4:19
- ☐ II Tim. 1:7
- ☐ Jn. 1:12
- ☐ Jn. 14:26-27
- ☐ Phil. 4:6-7

LESSON 2

The Basics of Contentment

Hebrews 13:5 says we are to, "...be content with _____
_____ _____ _____ _____...."

It is put even more plainly and in more basic terms, in I Timothy 6:8, "And having _____ and _____ let us be therewith content."

God says in that verse that there are two earthly basics with which we are to be content:

    1. _____

    2. _____ (clothing)

Read these two verses carefully:

(Psalm 23:1) "The Lord is my shepherd; I shall not _____."

(Psalm 34:10) "The young lions do _____, and suffer hunger: but they that seek the Lord shall not _____ any good thing."

_____

_____

_____

_____

Here are some tough questions:

1. If you had nothing but the clothes you are wearing and food to eat, would you be content?

2. Do you think that is even possible?

3. Are you content with the things you currently have?

"When we are discontent, we are acting on _____."

Eve's focus (Gen. 3) on the one thing she could not have instead of all the bounty God had given her opened her mind to temptation, and led to her disobedience. Satan often does the same to us. He turns our attention to that ONE THING we don't have, and tempts us to be bitter, to be ungrateful, even to be disobedient to God in order to acquire that one thing.

> *"Oh, what a happy soul am I! Although I cannot see,*
> *I am resolved that in this world Contented I will be.*
> *How many blessings I enjoy that other people don't*
> *To weep and sigh because I'm blind, I cannot, and I won't."*
>
> -Fanny Crosby, age 8

Assignment:

Answer these questions:

- Do I have food?
- Do I have clothing?

Stop today and take the time to thank God for your food and for your clothing. Each day this week, thank God for at least one material thing He has provided for you that exceeds these necessities. If you don't have it already, ask the Lord to help you develop an attitude of conscious gratitude. Be quick to give thanks to Him for His mercies and benefits, great and small.

Class Assignment:

Share one thing from the above list with those in your group. Be aware and appreciative to the Lord for His abundant blessings.

Memory Verse: "Blessed be the Lord, who daily loadeth us with benefits, even the God of our salvation. Selah." (Ps. 68:19).

13

Scripture Writing Challenge

- ☐ I Tim. 6:6-8
- ☐ Lk. 3:13-14
- ☐ Ps. 23:1
- ☐ Ps. 34:10
- ☐ Ps. 68:19

Bonus Challenge:

- ☐ Mt. 6:24-34

LESSON 3

The Boundaries of Contentment

Philippians 4:11 says that Paul had learned "…in _____ _____ _____ _____ therewith to be content."

The word "state" means "_____; _____."

The boundaries set forth in this passage are very broad:

- In _____ _____ (condition; circumstance) I am
- _____
- In _____ things

You may be thinking, "How can I possibly be content in all circumstances, in all places, for all things? That's impossible!" And in our own strength, it is.

Thankfully, the Holy Spirit answers our doubts and deficiencies in verse 13, "I can do _____ things through _____ which strengtheneth me."

(Pro. 30:8-9) "Remove far from me vanity and lies: give me neither _____ nor_____; feed me with food convenient for me: Lest I be _____, and _____ thee, and say, Who is the LORD? Or lest I be _____, and _____, and take the name of my God in _____."

15

Paul had learned how to deal with both of these extremes. He states,

"I know both how to be _____, and I know how to _____: _____ and in _____ things I am instructed both to be _____ and to be _____, both to _____ and to suffer _____." (Phil. 4:11-12)

How can we learn to deal with abundance or need with the same grace and peace that sustained Paul? The very next verse gives the answer:

"I can do _____ things through _____ which strengtheneth me."(Phil. 4:13)

Where was Paul when he penned the letter to the Philippians? _____

_____

Where was Eve when she fell for the temptation of Satan? _____

_____

Contentment is not based on your location or your circumstances. It is based on whose words you believe.

Class Assignment: Think about people in the Bible who tended to forget God in prosperity, but turned to Him in poverty or trouble. Make a list. Discuss the dangers of pride and prosperity, and the importance of learning faith and contentment in every circumstance of life.

Assignment 1:

Is there a place or a circumstance in which you are struggling to be content? Perhaps it is where you live, the time of life you are currently in, or a hardship you are currently experiencing. Write it down.

Ask the Lord to help you to learn to be content in that specific circumstance. When your heart seems to feel, "I can't!" respond with Philippians 4:13, "I can do all things through Christ which strengtheneth me."

Truth: *Many times, it is not that we cannot be content through Christ, it is that we will not. We have chosen in our hearts to be unthankful for a specific circumstance.*

Assignment 2:

Each day, thank God for the specific circumstance you are struggling with. Ask Him to teach you the lesson He would have you to learn through that specific "classroom" in your life. Praise Him for being with you in that circumstance.

Memory Verses: I know both how to be abased, and I know how to abound: every where and in all things I am instructed both to be full and to be hungry, both to abound and to suffer need. I can do all things through Christ which strengtheneth me." (Phil. 4:12-13)

Scripture Writing Challenge

- ☐ Phil. 4:4
- ☐ Phil. 4:10-13
- ☐ Phil. 4:18-19
- ☐ Pro. 30:8-9
- ☐ I Thes. 5:18

DISCONTENTMENT EXPOSED

Niki Lott

LESSON 4

The Barrier to Contentment

The Source of Discontent

Hebrews 13:5 says, "Let your conversation be without _____;
and be _____ with such things as ye have: for he hath said, I will
never leave thee, nor forsake thee."

In Ephesians 5:5 we read, "For this ye know, that no whoremonger, nor unclean
person, nor _____ man, who is an _____, hath any
inheritance in the kingdom of Christ and of God."

In Colossians 3:5 He says, "Mortify therefore your members which are upon the
earth; fornication, uncleanness, inordinate affection, evil concupiscence, and
_____, which is _____:"

**When we are not content with God's provision for us, it is because we
_____, _____, and _____ something other than God.
We are _____, perhaps not outwardly, but certainly in our
_____.**

Finish this statement in your own heart: "I need Jesus, and _____".

If there is anything but a period after the word "Jesus" in that sentence, we still
have a lot of learning to do. Perhaps there are some secret idols in our hearts.
Are we willing to tear them down and lay them at the feet of the Lord Jesus
Christ?

Class Assignment: List some things that are "good things" that can become idols to us — things that we tend to love, trust, or desire more than God. It can also be something that is keeping you from being content with God, His plan and provision in your life.

If there is anything on that list that you see in your own life, "tear it down" in your heart. Offer it to God as a sacrifice. Confess it as sin, and ask the Lord to teach you to worship, love, and serve Him alone.

Memory Verse: "Whom have I in heaven but thee? and there is none upon earth that I desire beside thee." (Ps. 73:25)

Scripture Writing Challenge

☐ I Tim. 6:9-10
☐ Eph. 5:5
☐ Col. 3:5

The Symptoms of Discontent

When we become covetous, there are certain symptoms that will become evident in our lives over time. It is possible to have some of these symptoms without having all of them, but having any of them should alert us that we are in spiritual danger.

- C_____ (I Tim. 6:9-10; Josh. 7:21)

- C_____ (I Tim. 6:9-10)

  "For where your _____ is, there will your _____ be also." (Mt. 6:21)

  Covetousness always comes back to the _____, and our relationship with the _____. Think of the question Jesus asked Peter three times: "Lovest thou me _____ than _____?" (Jn. 21:15-17)

  Do we love God more?

  More than what?

  More than anything. More than money. More than status. More than security. More than people. More than _____ (you fill in the blank). If there is anything we love and desire more than God, we need to ask the Lord to forgive us, and to help us to love Him most.

- C_____ (living for the things that please the flesh)

Niki Lott

(Lk. 12:15) "And he said unto them, Take heed, and _____ of covetousness: for a man's life consisteth not in the _____ of the _____ which he possesseth."

Jesus warns us to remember that life isn't about _____ we possess. No, rather it is about _____ we possess, and Who possesses us.

Jesus followed that warning with the parable about the rich man who laid up much treasure, but wasn't prepared for eternity. (Lk. 12:16-21) In very strong language, God calls this man a fool and again warns us, "So is he that layeth up treasure for _____, and is not rich toward _____." (Lk. 12:21).

- **C**_____ (slothfulness)

(Pro. 21:25-26) "The desire of the _____ killeth him; for his hands refuse to labour. He _____ greedily all the day long: but the righteous _____ and spareth not."

Proverbs has a great deal to say about the slothful person. We need to ask God to help us to have a content heart, but also a diligent _____ (Pro. 31:13). We should be willing to work, and to be good stewards of what God has entrusted to our care.

The Scripture above (Pro. 21:25-26) contrasts the covetous _____ of the slothful with the _____ of the righteous, "…the righteous giveth and spareth not." A good test for our level of contentment vs. covetousness might be how willing we are to give of what we have to others. Are we greedy and stingy, or are we "cheerful givers"?

- C_____

(II Cor. 10:12) "For we dare not make ourselves of the number, or _____ ourselves with some that commend themselves: but they _____ themselves by themselves, and _____ themselves among themselves, are _____ _____."

- C_____

(Num. 11:1a) "And when the people _____, it _____ the Lord: and the Lord heard it; and his _____was kindled…"

(See also I Cor. 10:1-12)

Class Assignment:

Consider this list of "symptoms". Can you think of any other Bible characters who struggled with these? How did it affect them spiritually? How did it affect others in their families/churches/communities?

- ☐ **Cravings**

- ☐ **Coldness**

- ☐ **Carnality**

- ☐ **Carelessness**

- ☐ **Comparing**

- ☐ **Complaining**

Personal Assignment:

Do a "spiritual checkup". Begin with the memory verses below as a prayer, then take the list of "symptoms" above and ask the Lord if any of them are in your life. If so, mark it, confess it to the Lord, and ask for His help in forsaking it.

Memory Verse: "Search me, O God, and know my heart: try me, and know my thoughts: And see if there be any wicked way in me, and lead me in the way everlasting." (Ps. 139:23-24).

Scripture Writing Challenge

- ☐ Josh. 7:21
- ☐ Mt. 6:21
- ☐ Jn. 21:15-17
- ☐ Lk. 12:15
- ☐ Pro. 21:25-26
- ☐ Pro. 31:13
- ☐ II Cor. 10:12
- ☐ Num. 11:1a
- ☐ Ps. 139:23-24

Niki Lott

CONTENTMENT EXPERIENCED

Niki Lott

LESSON 5

The Bewilderment of Contentment

The Paradox

A paradox is "a tenet contrary to received _____", or "a statement that is _____ contrary or opposed to common sense, and yet is perhaps _____" (*Merriam-Webster Dictionary*).

The spiritual life is full of such paradoxes - truths that seem to be contradictory to the natural mind. Here are a few examples:

- To live, we must _____. (Gal. 2:20)
- To be great, we must be _____. (Mt. 20:26-27)
- When we are weak, then we are _____. (II Cor. 12:10)
- To become wise, we must become as _____. (I Cor. 3:18)
- To be first, we must be _____. (Mt. 20:16)

The Christian who is "self-satisfied" may **appear** content.

The church of Laodicea described themselves in this way, "I am _____, and increased with _____, and have _____ of nothing..." (Rev. 3:17a) They were quite "content" with their condition.

God saw them as spiritually bankrupt.

He said to them, "...and _____ _____ that thou art wretched, and miserable, and _____, and _____, and naked:" (Rev. 3:17b)

Contentment is not a satisfaction in _____. It is a growing realization that I can find no _____ apart from Him and His perfect will.

Assignment:

Can you think of any other spiritual paradoxes?

Do you believe what God says about these truths?

Scripture Writing Challenge

- ☐ Gal. 2:20
- ☐ Mt. 20:26-27
- ☐ II Cor. 12:10
- ☐ I Cor. 3:18
- ☐ Mt. 20:16
- ☐ Phil. 3:10

Memory Verse: (Gal. 2:20) "I am crucified with Christ: nevertheless I live; yet not, I, but Christ liveth in me: and the life which I now live in the flesh I live by the faith of the Son of God, who loved me, and gave himself for me."

The Passion

These verses in the Psalms demonstrate this type of passion and desire for God: "As the hart _____ after the water brooks, so _____ my soul after thee, O God. My soul _____ for _____ for the living God: when shall I come and appear before God?" (Ps. 42:1-2)

"O God, thou art my God; early will I _____ thee: my soul _____ for thee, my flesh _____ for thee in a dry and thirsty land, where no water is; To see thy power and thy glory, so as I have seen thee in the sanctuary. Because thy lovingkindness is better than _____, my lips shall praise thee." (Ps. 63:1-3)

Consider these words of Job: "Neither have I gone back from the commandment of his lips; I have esteemed the _____ of his mouth more than my _____food." (Job 23:12)

Over and over, the Bible reminds us that God's Word and wisdom are more to be desired than _____ and _____. While most of the human race covet temporal things, the child of God who learns contentment in things of this world will learn to desire spiritual and eternal things. (Ps. 19:7-10; Pro. 8:11)

 **Assignment:**

How is your passion and desire for God?

Are you satisfied with where you are spiritually, or do you desire more?

Is there a specific area of your walk with the Lord where you have a strong desire to grow and to learn?

Based on what you have written here, take the time to pray specifically and fervently for these requests, and don't forget to thank God!

 **Scripture Writing Challenge**

☐ Ps. 42:1-2
☐ Ps. 63:1-3
☐ Job 23:12
☐ Ps. 19:7-10
☐ Pro. 8:11

The Parting

"If any man teach otherwise, and consent not to _____ words, even the words of our Lord _____ _____, and to the _____ which is according to godliness; He is _____, knowing nothing, but doting about _____ and strifes of words, whereof cometh _____, strife, railings, evil surmisings, Perverse disputings of men of _____ minds, and destitute of the _____, supposing that _____ is _____: from such _____ thyself. But _____ with _____ is great _____." (I Tim. 3:3-6)

God gives a strong warning about false teachers who "...through _____ shall they with feigned words make _____ of you: whose _____ now of a long time lingereth not, and their damnation slumbereth not." (II Pet. 2:1-3)

Covetousness is _____ and it _____.

Spiritual _____ requires that we exercise spiritual _____.

(I Tim. 6:9-10) "They that will be _____..." – those who desire to be rich in the things of this world – "...fall into temptation and a _____, and into many foolish and hurtful _____, which drown men in destruction and perdition. For the _____ of money is the root of all evil: which while some _____ after, they have erred from the _____, and pierced themselves through with many sorrows."

God clearly admonishes us to beware of covetousness. He tells us to _____, and then to _____, from those who are going down this path.

He first says, "from such _____ thyself" (I Tim. 6:5), and then says, "..._____ these things..." (I Tim. 6:11)

We must remember that it is not enough to just separate from the company of those with these attitudes. We must search out and sever those attitudes from our own hearts.

The greatest danger we face is not the temptation from _____, but the temptation _____.

Assignment:

Do you love money, or the power and influence it can buy?

Have you been tempted to believe the lie that material "blessings" are proof of someone's spirituality?

Are you being influenced (through books, media, friendships, etc.) by those who do believe this type of thinking?

If yes, what are you going to do about it? How can you "part" from this thinking and influence in your life?

Scripture Writing Challenge

- ☐ I Tim. 6:3-6
- ☐ II Pet. 2:1-3

LESSON 6
The Beauty of Contentment

The Pursuit

"…and _____ after righteousness, godliness, faith, love, patience, meekness." (I Tim. 6:11)

God doesn't just tell us what to run _____, but also what to run _____. He tells us that as we flee the dangers of covetousness and false doctrine in our lives, we are free to pursue the godly qualities that will bring us true contentment, joy, and blessings in our lives. What are these qualities?

- **Righteousness - our _____ with God**

  Our righteousness is only and always a result of the work of God in our lives, and the relationship and fellowship we have with Him.

  Righteousness is placed _____ upon us by God _____ salvation (II Tim. 3:16; Rom. 4:2-6, 20-25; Isa. 61:10; Rom. 10:3-13, 17; Gal. 2:20-21; Phil. 3:9)

  Righteousness does not _____ salvation; it is the _____ of salvation. (Isa. 64:6)

It is not a _____ we obtain salvation; it is the _____ of obtaining salvation.

Righteousness is placed upon us at salvation by God's _____ through _____ in Jesus Christ. (Eph. 2:8-10)

Righteousness is _____ in us by God _____ salvation.

How can we have righteousness not only positionally, but practically, in our daily lives? God produces the fruit of righteousness in our lives:

- Through _____ in God's Word (Phil. 3:9; Rom. 1:17; 10:17)
- Through yielded _____ to God's Word (Rom. 8:4-6; Rom. 6:9-19)

Righteousness should be _____ _____ for God _____ salvation. (I Tim. 6:11; II Tim. 2:22)

Throughout the Bible, righteousness is compared to clothing.

Name some of these comparisons:

- a _____ (Job 29:14; Isa. 61:10)
- a _____ (Isa. 59:17; Eph. 6:14)
- a _____ _____ (Ps. 132:9).

Righteousness is to be a visible covering that _____ our lives and _____ the Lord.

What are some of the things found in Ephesians 4 that we are to "put off" and "put on" as the children of righteousness?

- We are to "put off" the _____ man and put on the _____ man. (vs. 22, 24)
- We are to "put away" _____ and speak _____. (vs. 25)

- We are to be _____ and sin _____. (vs. 26)
- We are not to give _____ to the _____. (vs. 27)
- We are not to _____, but instead to _____ with our hands, that we may _____ to those in need. (vs. 28)
- We are not to let _____ communication proceed out of our mouth, but instead are to speak words that are _____ and filled with grace. (vs. 29)
- We are not to _____ the Holy Spirit. (vs. 30)
- We are to put away _____, _____, _____, _____, evil _____, and _____, and instead we are to be _____, _____, and _____. (vs. 31-32)

God promises that those who hunger and thirst for righteousness will be _____. (Mt. 5:6)

Assignment:

When did you receive the righteousness of God (when did you trust Christ as your Savior)?

Are you actively seeking to live a righteous and holy life, both inwardly and outwardly?

Are there any areas where you could "put on" the garments of righteousness?

If there is unrighteousness in our lives, we can claim the promise found in I John 1:9. Write that promise here:

Scripture Writing Challenge

- ☐ I Tim. 6:11
- ☐ Phil. 3:9
- ☐ Tit. 3:5
- ☐ Isa. 64:6
- ☐ Tit. 2:12
- ☐ II Tim. 3:16
- ☐ Isa. 61:10
- ☐ Gal. 2:20-21

- ☐ Eph. 2:8-10
- ☐ Rom. 1:17
- ☐ II Tim. 2:22
- ☐ Job 29:14
- ☐ Ps. 132:9
- ☐ Mt. 5:6
- ☐ Isa. 59:17
- ☐ Eph. 6:14

Bonus Challenge:

- ☐ Rom. 10:3-13, 17
- ☐ Rom. 8:4-6
- ☐ Rom. 6:9-19
- ☐ Eph. 4:25-32

- **Godliness – Our _____ of God**

Godliness is our _____ _____ toward God that
expresses itself in our _____ _____. It is a _____
of _____ that is reflected in the _____ of our _____.
It is the _____ of God's _____ _____ out in good
_____. It is the light that _____ before men in such a way
that while they _____ our good works, they _____ our
great God. (Mt. 5:16)

It is easy to think that we cannot truly live a godly life in the corrupt
culture in which we live. It is easy to believe that we must be like the
world in order to win the world. However, neither of those thoughts are
true.

Consider the following verses:

"For the _____ of God that bringeth _____
hath appeared to all men, _____ us that, denying
_____ and worldly _____, we should
live _____, _____, and _____,
in this _____ world;" (Tit. 2:11-12)

Assignment:

Would your family, friends, and neighbors describe you as a godly person – not religious, but godly?

Are there any areas of "ungodliness and worldly lusts" that need to be denied in your life?

What are some of the ways that we can learn to have, and display, the mind of Christ (Phil. 2:1-11)? Try to name at least five.

Scripture Writing Challenge

- ☐ I Tim. 2:10
- ☐ II Cor. 5:15
- ☐ Rom. 6:10-11 (*omit if already done in previous bonus section)

Bonus Challenge:

- ☐ Phil. 2:1-11

- **Faith – Our _____ upon God**

  - **Genuine faith is clear in its _____.**

    We are clearly instructed and often reminded to have faith in _____. (Mk. 11:22) We must be careful to keep our faith firmly fixed on the right object – our unchanging _____ and His perfect _____. (Gal. 3:26; II Tim. 3:16; Rom. 10:17)

  - **Genuine faith is clear in its _____. (Jas. 1:22)**

  Assignment:

  Consider the object and obedience of your faith. Is your faith founded on God and His Word?

What if the Word of God contradicts popular opinion, or your own thinking? Is there an area in your life that this is true? How are you responding?

Are you actively, intentionally obeying the Word of God?

Scripture Writing Challenge

☐ Pro. 3:5-7
☐ Heb. 10:38
☐ Mk. 11:22
☐ Rom. 10:17
☐ Jas. 1:22

Bonus Challenge:

☐ Heb. 11:1-6

- **Love – Our** _____ **of God to others**

Christ's love _____. **Our love** _____.

"We _____ Him, because He _____ loved us." (I Jn. 4:19)

Christ's love _____. **Our love** _____ (Rom. 8:35-39; Zeph. 3:17).

Christ's love _____. *Our love* _____.
(Rom. 8:37; I Cor. 13:8)

His love allows us to conquer _____ (I Jn. 4:18), and to conquer sin.

Genuine love does not rejoice in _____or sin, but rejoices in _____ (I Cor. 13:6).

Christ's love _____. **Our love** _____.
(II Cor. 5:14)

When we love Christ as we should, we gladly relinquish our love for the _____ and the things in it (I Jn. 2:15).

This love for Him also teaches us to relinquish our selfish desires and rights in order to love those around us (Rom. 12:10).

Christ's love _____. **Our love** _____.
(Jn. 17:26; Eph. 4:15)

As I John 3:18 says, "My little children, let us not love in _____, neither in _____; but in _____ and in _____."

Our _____ (v. 1), our _____ (v.2), and even our _____ (v. 3) are meaningless if they are not motivated by charity (I Cor. 13:1-3).

Christ's love _____. **Our love** _____.

47

"If ye _____ me, _____ my commandments." (Jn. 14:15).

Our keeping of His commandments is not about somehow _____ His love; it is _____ of our love. It is not a means of _____ His love, but of _____ ours.

How do we know if we love God? It is not by how we feel, or by what we say, but by whether or not we obey His words.

"For this is the _____ of God, that we keep his _____: and his commandments are not _____." (I Jn. 5:3)

The commandment to love God with all that we are is the greatest commandment and should be the greatest aim of our lives. Our love for God should surpass and supersede every other love in our lives. It must be greater than our love for self, our love for our friends, and even our love for our families. This love for God should be the motivating factor in everything we do and say.

As our love grows and matures, it will be evidenced and expressed in our _____ to be in His presence, our _____ to keep His commandments, and our _____ before and to others.

This love will flow in spiritual order:

1. It will commence in our _____ as we fellowship consistently with Him.
2. It will continue in our _____ as we decide to fully commit to Him.
3. It will be completed in our _____ as we follow His commandments and meet the needs of others.

Assignment:

Read I Corinthians 13. Wherever the word "charity" is used, insert your name. This isn't to try to change the Scripture but to help us to realize the personal attitudes and actions that God wants to develop in our lives as we love Him and others. Are there any specific areas where God needs to teach you to love as He does?

Challenge Assignment:

Find and read the book, *If,* by Amy Carmichael.

If you do not order a copy to read, search for quotes from it online. Write down at least three quotes that cause you to think about how you can have a more Christlike love.

Scripture Writing Challenge

- [ ] I Jn. 3:16-18
- [ ] Zeph. 3:17
- [ ] II Cor. 5:14
- [ ] I Jn. 2:3-5, 15-17
- [ ] Jn. 17:26
- [ ] Eph. 4:15

- [ ] Rom. 5:5, 8
- [ ] Jn. 13:34-35
- [ ] Jn. 15:12, 17
- [ ] I Thes. 3:2
- [ ] Jn. 14:15
- [ ] I Jn. 5:2-3

Bonus Challenge:

- [ ] Rom. 8:35-39
- [ ] I Jn. 4:7-12; 16-21
- [ ] I Cor. 13

- **Patience – Our** _____ **that God's will is perfect**

Patience comes as a result of the _____, or testing, of our faith. Patience is a work God does in our lives to _____ and complete us. Patience is quietly, calmly _____ hardship and trials. It is being willing to wait _____, without complaint, for God's timing. It is gentle _____ with those who are not so gentle or forbearing toward us. It is _____ continuance, despite opposition or even persecution.

Just as we must let God's peace rule in our lives, so we must _____ His patience _____ in our lives (Jas. 1:2-4).

Assignment:

In what areas is God testing your faith?

Are you letting patience work? Sometimes we fight the process. Can you identify any ways that you may be keeping patience from having her perfect work in your life?

Many times when we don't "let patience have her perfect work", covetousness can creep in. Read Psalm 37. What are some of the dangers, or demonstrations, of resisting the work of patience?

Scripture Writing Challenge

☐ Jas. 1:2-4
☐ I Pet. 4:12-13
☐ Ps. 37:7

- **Meekness - our _____ to God and others**

Meekness is _____, yielded, obedient, and content. It is a defining quality of someone who has yielded _____ in their life to the Spirit of God, and has found Him to be the source of their _____ and their _____.

Paul said, "I know both how to be abased, and I know how to abound…" (Phil. 4:12)

In II Cor. 10:1 he said, "Now I Paul myself beseech you by the _____ and gentleness of Christ, who in presence am base among you…"

Why should we want to follow after meekness?

- Because meek people have yielded control of themselves to God, He often entrusts them with _____. (Num. 12:3)
- Because meek people have yielded their desires to God, He promises they will be _____. (Ps. 22:26)
- Because meek people view themselves honestly through the mirror of God's Word, they have no illusions about themselves and do not depend on themselves for guidance, and so God promises to _____ them. (Ps. 25:9)
- Because meek people are willing to admit their utter dependence on God and their lack of wisdom, He promises to _____ them. (Ps. 25:9)
- Because meek people have relinquished their rights on this earth to God, He promises them an inheritance and _____. (Ps. 37:11; Mt. 5:5)
- Because meek people are not insistent on living for their own pleasure, God promises to increase their _____. (Isa. 29:19)

One of the sweetest, yet rarely talked about, attributes of our Lord Jesus Christ is His meekness. He who could rightfully demand the multitudes to worship on their faces came to this earth "_____ and lowly in heart" (Mt. 11:29; 21:5; II Cor. 10:1).

Oh, that we would heed this admonition, "Let this _____ be in you, which was also in Christ Jesus:" (Phil. 2:5)! What a difference it will make in our daily lives if we will be willing to let Him teach us to be meek.

- We will have _____ in our souls. (Mt. 11:29)
- We will have His help in restoring the _____. (II Tim. 2:25; Gal. 6:1)
- We will reflect His _____. (Gal. 5:22-23; Col. 3:12-13; Eph. 4:1-3)
- We will receive His _____ and wisdom. (Jas. 1:21)
- We will reveal His _____, His _____, His grace, and His glory. (Jas. 3:13; I Pet. 3:4, 15; Jas. 3:13-18; Tit. 3:2-6)

"Blessed are the _____..." (Mt. 5:5)

Memory Verse: (I Tim. 6:11) "But thou, O man of God, flee these things; and follow after righteousness, godliness, faith, love, patience, meekness."

Assignment:

Meekness is often mischaracterized by the world as weakness. In truth, it is characterized by two great qualities: humility and surrender. The Bible says we are to take His yoke upon us and learn of Him, for He is meek and lowly in heart. Consider your heart. Does it reflect these qualities?

Have you taken His yoke, surrendered your will to His control? Have you chosen to follow His lead, to humbly labor and serve alongside Him?

Study the meekness of Christ. Think on it. How could you learn and practice meekness from His example?

Scripture Writing Challenge

☐ II Tim. 2:24-26   ☐ Mt. 11:29
☐ I Pet. 3:4   ☐ Mt. 21:5
☐ Tit. 3:2   ☐ Gal. 6:1
☐ Eph. 4:1-3   ☐ Gal. 5:22-23
☐ Num. 12:3   ☐ Col. 3:12-13
☐ Isa. 29:19   ☐ Jas. 1:21

Bonus Challenge:

☐ Jas. 3:13-18
☐ Tit. 3:2-6

Niki Lott

LESSON 7

The Benefit of Contentment

This lesson teaches us the "_____" of contentment.

"But _____ with _____ is great
_____." (I Tim. 6:5-7; Pro. 28:16)

The "gain" spoken of in this verse doesn't refer to some financial or material reward. We know this for certain because the Scripture says, "For we brought _____ into this world, and it is certain we can carry _____ out." (I Tim. 6:7)

Understanding and practicing God's _____ about gain frees us from the snare and ensuing _____ of materialism and _____. When we are free from the notion that _____ things can somehow bring us _____, it is then that we gain the joy, the blessings, and the rewards that come from pursuing and enjoying that which is _____. (II Cor. 4:18; Col. 3:1-3)

Let's take a brief look at God's perspective of gain:

What Isn't Gain	What Is Gain
A good _____ (Phil. 3:4-7)	_____ (Pro. 3:13-14; 8:11, 19; 16:16)
_____ without godliness (Ps. 37:16; Pro. 10:2; 11:4; 16:8)	Godliness with _____ (I Tim. 6:5-7)
A good _____ (Phil. 3:4-7)	A good _____ (Pro. 22:1)
_____; morality (Phil. 3:4-7)	The knowledge, fellowship, & _____ of Christ (Phil. 3:7-10)
Focusing on the temporal, not the _____ (Mt. 16:26; Jas. 4:13)	_____ in Christ (Phil. 1:21)
Earthly possessions with an _____ family (Pro. 15:27)	A happy _____, even with poverty (Pro. 15:16-17; 16:8)
The "great" words of _____ (II Pet. 2:18-19; Jude 1:16)	The Word of _____ (Ps. 19:10; 119:72, 127)
Physical health & bodily _____ (Phil. 3:3; I Tim. 4:8)	Spiritual _____ (Phil. 3:7-8; I Tim. 4:8)

True contentment springs from a heart that has set its _____ on God. (Ps. 73:25-26; Phil. 3:7-10) Is God enough? When we learn that He truly is all we need, we will realize genuine spiritual contentment.

Class Assignment:

Consider the world's perspective of what is "gain", or what is profitable and valuable, vs. God's perspective. What are some practical ways that God's perspective on gain should change our lives as believers?

What is the number one takeaway you have from this study on contentment?

Memory Verse: (I Tim. 6:6) "But godliness with contentment is great gain."

Scripture Writing Challenge

- [ ] Phil. 3:3-7
- [ ] Pro. 28:16
- [ ] Col. 3:1-3
- [ ] II Cor. 4:18
- [ ] Pro. 3:13-14
- [ ] Pro. 8:11, 19
- [ ] Pro. 16:8, 16
- [ ] Ps. 37:16
- [ ] Pro. 10:2
- [ ] Pro. 11:4
- [ ] Pro. 22:1
- [ ] Mt. 16:26
- [ ] Jas. 4:13
- [ ] Phil. 1:21
- [ ] Pro. 15:16-17, 27
- [ ] II Pet. 2:18-19
- [ ] Jude 16
- [ ] Ps. 19:10
- [ ] Ps. 119:72, 127
- [ ] I Tim. 4:8

www.ingramcontent.com/pod-product-compliance
Lightning Source LLC
Chambersburg PA
CBHW020606030426
42337CB00013B/1236